CHEF

DOUGLAS BENDER

People I Meet

A Crabtree Roots Book

Crabtree Publishing
crabtreebooks.com

School-to-Home Support for Caregivers and Teachers

This book helps children grow by letting them practice reading. Here are a few guiding questions to help the reader with building his or her comprehension skills. Possible answers appear here in red.

Before Reading:

- What do I think this book is about?
    - *I think this book is about working in a restaurant.*
    - *I think this book is about chefs.*
- What do I want to learn about this topic?
    - *I want to learn more about how chefs make delicious food.*
    - *I want to learn how to make my favorite foods.*

During Reading:

- I wonder why...
    - *I wonder why a chef wears a tall white hat.*
    - *I wonder why chefs use different-sized pots.*
- What have I learned so far?
    - *I have learned that chefs cook in kitchens.*
    - *I have learned that chefs can make many different kinds of food.*

After Reading:

- What details did I learn about this topic?
    - *I have learned that chefs can make many kinds of desserts.*
    - *I have learned that chefs usually wear white clothes.*
- Read the book again and look for the vocabulary words.
    - *I see the word **kitchen** on page 6 and the word **desserts** on page 10. The other vocabulary words are found on page 14.*

This is a **chef**.

Chefs can make many kinds of **food**.

This chef is in a **kitchen**.

Chefs use big and little **pots**.

Chefs can make many kinds of **desserts** too.

I like to eat food made by a chef!

Word List

Sight Words

a	eat	little	this
and	in	made	to
big	is	make	too
by	kinds	many	use
can	like	of	

Words to Know

chef

desserts

food

kitchen

pots